STEVENS F.C.

Michael Rosen
Illustrated by John Rogan

(Helped by Eddie Rosen)

Why isn't my name on the cover, Dad?

Writing's a cruel game, son.

ABOUT THE AUTHOR

Michael Rosen is a poet, an author of popular children's books, an entertainer and radio and tv personality, who is known for his wonderful picture books and hilarious poetry collections.

Michael lives in London, where he was born and is a passionate football supporter. Currently he is the Children's Laureate.

OTHER BARN OWL BOOKS BY MICHAEL ROSEN

You're Thinking About Doughnut
You're Thinking About Tomatoes

BARN OWL BOOKS

157 Fortis Green Road, London, N10 3LX
www.barnowlbooks.com

First published in 1995 by A & C Black in hardback
And Harper Collins in paperback

This edition published by Barn Owl Books, 2008
157 Fortis Green Road, London, N10 3LX

Distributed by Frances Lincoln,
4 Torriano Mews, Torriano Avenue, London, NW5 2RZ

Text copyright © Michael Rosen 1995, 2008
Illustrations copyright © John Rogan 1995, 2008

The moral rights of the author
and illustrator have been asserted

ISBN 978 19 0 301571 1

Designed and typeset by Skandesign Ltd
Produced in Poland by Polskabook

We have been unable to trace John Rogan and would very much appreciate anyone who could help us make contact with him.

Chapter 1

Wayne Travis was football mad.
So were most of his friends.

Every day at school, they played 23-a-side
football in the space round by the dustbins.
No ref, one goal.

Wayne's ambition was to be a professional footballer. Every day he watched his *Goals of the Century* video and imagined being on television.

What Wayne imagined…

…this free kick is on the halfway line. McGimpsey runs into open space. Travis steps up and it's a high swirling ball aimed at the big target man but no, yes, incredible, it's a GOAL!…

Wayne's other ambition was to perfect the famous Hedley Carlton Triple-Bounce-Goal, as described to him by his grandad.

I shall never forget that goal. It wasn't just the swerve; it wasn't just the speed; each bounce zig-zagged across the pitch as if the ball had a life of its own.

Wayne decided to have a go. His foot
swerved as it approached the ball, then
spun back the other way. At the same
time it flipped up under the ball.

The result was amazing.
The ball flew like a rocket
towards Shaheed.

It dipped, bounced,
swerved off towards
Roger and Harry.

It bounced again and swerved back
towards the two Shonas.

It bounced again and headed for
Maxine and Lara.

Then it hurtled into the goal,
hitting the wall with a thunderous wham.

I've done a
Hedley Carlton
Triple-Bounce
Goal!

From then on, Wayne practised the foot
move whenever he could. Under the
table, on the bus, at breakfast...
swerve, spin-back, flip-up.
Swerve, spin-back, flip-up.

Chapter 2

Wayne wasn't the only one in his family who liked football. On Saturday mornings Wayne's dad played for a team called Even Stevens.

Everyone in the team lived in Shakespeare Street. It was called Even Stevens because all the players lived in houses or flats with even numbers. They played their matches on the Astroturf behind the Mammoth Hypermarket.

EVEN STEVENS F.C.
Team Notes

(nicknames in brackets)

Starting from top left...

Erkan Hussein, 21. Leather worker. Excellent right foot, terrible left. Mother works at Tesco. **(Tesco)**

Harry Postlethwaite, 52. Bus driver. Terrible right foot, terrible left foot. Says he knew Sir Stanley Matthews. **(Stan)**

Darren Stewart, 13. School kid. Brilliant all-rounder. Only one eye. **(Nelson)**

Chuck Bradley, 35. Unemployed. Ex-American football player. **(Superbowl)**

Moira Stewart, 41. Darren's mum, ex-Scotland ladies team. **(Jock)**

Satoshi Watanabe, 20. Student. Broke Tokyo record for spinning a basketball on one finger. **(Guinness)**

Solly Rosenberg, 68. Once captained United London Jewish Boys clubs tour of Wales. **(Taffy)**

Linton Harper, 19. Computer salesman. Rap artist, team kit style consultant. Wikkid! **(Mr Kool)**

Linford Harper, 21. Linton's older brother. Bosses him around something shocking. **(Bossman)**

Nigel Fiddle, 18. Shoe shop assistant. Awful player, but can get football boots dead cheap. **(Start-rite)**

Rodney Travis, 38. Wayne's dad. Bad back, bad right knee, bad shoulder, bad neck. Part-time postman. **(Pat)**

Salvatore Delgado, 16. Claims to be grandson of reserve team member in 1970 world-cup winning Brazil squad. **(Pele)**

Donna Louis, 16. Ex-spectator of Linton. Now plays in her own right. **(Mrs Kool)**

One Friday night in September, Erkan called round to see Wayne's dad.

Guess what, Pat, we're eligible for the F.A. Cup. The draw's just come through and we're up against Wealdstone next Saturday!

"Wealdstone?" said Wayne's dad. "But they're a really brilliant side, with ex-professionals. We'll be smashed."

Erkan wasn't put off. He told all the
members of the team the good news.
But there were a few problems.

For one thing, Nigel Fiddle
was in Latvia buying a
stock of cheap shoes,
so he wouldn't be
able to play.

For another, Wayne's
dad now had a bad
left knee, so he
wouldn't be able
to play either.

Chapter 3

Undaunted, that Saturday Erkan led Even Stevens F.C. out to play Wealdstone on the Astroturf behind the Mammoth Hypermarket.

And in that team was young Wayne Travis.

For everyone in Shakespeare Street it was a huge thrill, but no one else took much notice, except for a woman from the local radio station who happened to be passing.

It turned out to be scoop of the year for local radio.

Wealdstone's attack has been kept at bay by some extraordinary long-ball bouncing-passes by young Wayne Travis. They've just conceded a penalty in the 89th minute.

13-year-old Darren Stewart is taking the kick. He runs up… It's a goal! And there's the final whistle! Wealdstone have been beaten in the first qualifying round of the F.A. Cup!

Back in the dressing room (Moira Stewart's front room) Darren explained.

The goalie was watching my face and not the ball. So I leered at him with my false eye and he went the wrong way.

Chapter 4

The next day, Wayne and the rest of the team all tuned in to the local radio to hear the draw for the next round:

...versus Hendon
Bishop Auckland versus
    Corinthian Casuals
Cartilege United versus
    Even Stevens
Pinner versus...

Yeees! Yeeeaaa! Cartilege United! Didn't we beat them 4-nil only a few months back?

Meanwhile, in a garden shed somewhere in Enfield, Cartilege United were not so happy…

And so Even Stevens didn't have to play anyone at all in the next round of the F.A. Cup!

Chapter 5

Successfully through the qualifying rounds, their next challenge was to play the non-league professionals. They were drawn away against the powerful Telford United.

HACKNEY MERCURY

ON THE BALL
with Chris Hack

Young Wayne Travis is on top of the world. Just 9 years old, he's in the country's greatest football tournament.

'It's brill', states Wayne from his home in Shakespeare Street.

'His mum would've been proud of him,' adds Dad Rodney (38) part-time postman and widower.

And what of the amazing long-ball triple-bouncing passes we saw in the game?

'Just a fluke,' says fair-haired Wayne. 'I don't want to make too much of it.'

But it's certainly a RED LETTER day for Postman Dad!!!

When the big day came, Wayne's dad's knees were still playing up and Nigel was still in Latvia (or was it Poland?) So Wayne was in the team.

On the coach to Telford, Erkan dished out advice.

(*Wayne now had his own nickname, thanks to the Hedley Carlton Triple-Bounce.)

On the coach back from Telford...

By the time the coach got back to Hackney, the crowds were out to welcome them.

Chapter 6

Next day, the draw for the first round of the F.A. Cup took place on T.V.

...Even Stevens versus Blackpool...

Old Harry Postlethwaite couldn't believe his ears.

I don't believe it! That's Stanley Matthews' old team. When he beat...

...Bolton Wanderers single-handed in the 1953 cup final!

Will I get to play?

Wayne needn't have worried.

"We need you, Zig-zag," shouted Satoshi. "No one can read your game."

The Astroturf at the back of the Mammoth Hypermarket had never known anything like it. The car park was converted into a terrace and the local printer was selling programmes.

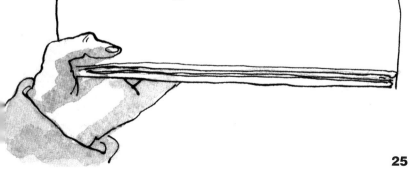

EVEN STEVENS

Official Programme
Price 50p

Even Stevens v Blackpool FC
(featuring Wayne 'Zig-zag' Travis)

FA Cup First Round

Every child and teacher from Wayne's school was there – even the head.

The whole nation tuned in to hear the report at the end of Grandstand.

ROUND 1

Two seconds into the game the non-leaguers were 1-nil down. It appeared to be a walk-over for the one-time cup-winning club of the great Sir Stanley Matthews.

But how that mighty name suffered today, as Blackpool experienced four early send-offs for unclean tackling!

With Blackpool down to seven men, Even Stevens were in with a chance. But Blackpool had further surprises in store, when four forwards formed a Rugby scrum and charged towards the goal with the ball tucked under one of their jerseys. Early bath for them too, and Blackpool were down to three men.

Even Stevens equalised after half time.
And then, in what must be one of the
upsets of the century, young Wayne Travis
took control of the ball.

Kicked from well outside Blackpool's
penalty area, the ball made an astonishing
triple-bouncing journey up the pitch.
I couldn't really see from where I was, but
somehow or other it landed up in the
Blackpool net.

At the final whistle it was 2-1 to Even Stevens. They're into round two, and they'll be celebrating down in Hackney tonight, I can tell you.

That night was the greatest night of
Wayne's life and he ate two kebabs,
fourteen Jaffa cakes,

four Jamaican patties,

eight slices of celebration cake,
fourteen packets of crisps

and twelve chocolate bars

at the celebration party
in Shakespeare Street.

Chapter 7

The next draw turned out to be against non-league Waterloo Station Rovers – what a let-down! It would have been much more fun to be beaten by one of the league teams.

Wayne went back to playing 23-a-side football in the alley behind school. He didn't practise his Hedley Carlton Triple-Bounce Goal.

A few weeks later, while Wayne was doing his homework and Dad was dozing in the armchair…

…semi-professional football club, Waterloo Station Rovers, has been forced to close down… in a statement… fraud… fifty thousand pounds missing… in court tomorrow… punched the manager… police… no further part in the F.A. Cup.

Wayne's dad woke up and leapt to his feet so suddenly that he put his back out.

That means we're through the second round of the F.A. Cup! If only I could get myself fit in time.

At first Wayne thought – brilliant!
Playing one of the big boys.

But then he thought…

Wouldn't that mean he'd lose his place
in the team? And hadn't Nigel Fiddle rung
from Poland (or Bulgaria) the other day
to say he was on his way back with a
lorry load of new shoes and boots?

Chapter 8

When Even Stevens were drawn away against Manchester United in the third round, even Moira Stewart was stunned to silence.

Manchester United?
    Old Trafford?
A crowd of over forty thousand?
        Live coverage on T.V?

Maybe they should simply bow out now before nerves and humiliation got the better of them.

Instead, what happened was one of the most curious and extraordinary games of football in the world.

Erkan Hussein may not have been the world's greatest captain, but he knew a thing or two about football. In the weeks leading up to the game he racked his brains and, by the day of the Big Match, he had a plan.

In the dressing room at Old Trafford he revealed it for the first time.

(He drew it in the steam on the dressing room window.)

As the teams ran out on to the pitch, the roar that hit them nearly knocked Wayne over. He was on the subs bench today, next to his dad who had a bad toe. (Nigel, who was back from Romania, had said, "Either I play or you lot don't get the new boots.")

Then came the Erkan Hussein plan.

...an amazing sight here at Old Trafford. The non-leaguers are in a semi-circle guarding their own goal. The United forwards are trying to fight their way through, but there really is no way round this.

Man. United's captain has called a
conference...

...And Even Stevens have broken out of
the semi-circle. They're taking the ball
upfield... and they've scored! And Man.
United haven't even noticed. What an
amazing move!

And 1-nil was where the score stayed until the final whistle. One of the smallest clubs in the world had beaten one of the biggest.

That night the World Football Council had an emergency meeting in the Eiffel Tower and changed the rules of football so that it could never happen again.

Rule Number 457
Semi circles and defences.
Teams are not allowed to form a defensive ring round the goal.

Chapter 9

Even Stevens were through to Round 4, away to Bristol Rovers. It was never going to be an easy game after the scandal at Old Trafford.

Look at this, Dad.

THE

SCUM

EVEN CHEATERS *CHEATS!!!*

Dirty, cheating crooks, Even Stevens, go to Bristol today and let's hope they get well and truly crushed.

Beat the Cheats!!

Football's a cruel game, son.

But Wayne was back in the team. (Nigel Fiddle had to go back to Romania – or was it Estonia? He had forgotten to pick up the boot-laces.)

Two minutes into the game, Bristol's Jimmy Rack left the field.

...Bristol Rovers will not be fielding any substitutes today: David Dover's wife, Eileen, has gone into hospital to have a baby and David's with her. Best of luck Eileen! And – amazing coincidence – Doug Bitnearer's wife is having a baby, too – best of luck Lena!

Three minutes later, three more went...

Well, here's a turn up for the books. Jimmy Rack's missus, Anna, has just been taken to hospital. They're expecting their third child. Best of luck Anna!

One minute later…

Dennis Pond's wife, Lily,
George Showers' wife, April, and
Pete Bee's wife, May, have all just been
taken to hospital to have their babies.

Well, there's certainly going to be a
few more little Rovers in town tonight.
Good luck Laura Norder, Ruby Redd
and the rest…!

Bristol Rovers were down to one man.
Even Stevens won 45-nil.

Chapter 10

Even Stevens were through to the fifth round of the F.A. Cup, with only sixteen clubs left in. Life was supposed to go on just as usual for the players, but it wasn't easy.

Erkan's leather factory started making leather badges:

Satoshi regularly appeared on satellite T.V. to Japan.

Linton was Number 1 in the Rap Charts with *Believin' Even Stevens.*

And Wayne…?   Well, the whole school was doing a project on football.

Even Stevens featured in the papers almost every day.

*SCUM*sport

FA CUP FIFTH ROUND
Win the pools with Harry Bigforest

WIMBLEDON V EVEN STEVENS
This should be a pushover for Wimbledon. Their superior long ball game should easily penetrate the non-leaguer's defence, though Stevens' captain, 'Tesco' Hussein tells me he's got something special up his sleeve (and it's not just his arm).

And indeed he had. When Even Stevens ran out on to the pitch for the game, everything looked normal.

But the moment the whistle blew, Even Stevens turned their backs on the Wimbledon goal and played the whole game running backwards.

Wimbledon's Greg Walnut tackled Moira.

The ref blew him up for tackling from behind.

Ron Cobnut tackled Donna.

The ref blew him up for tackling from behind.

It was unbeatable.
Wimbledon were completely outplayed.

FINAL SCORE:
Wimbledon 0, Even Stevens 3

That night the World Football Council had an emergency meeting at Niagara Falls:

Rule Number 458
Running backwards.
No team shall spend more than two minutes running, shooting, passing or playing set-pieces backwards.

Chapter 11

Even Stevens were through to the last eight.

Moira was a guest on breakfast television, and Linton appeared in a quiz show. Every single member of the team was involved in something, from opening supermarkets to charity work.

Wayne was finding it hard to concentrate in school.

...the capital of Egypt is Even Stevens ...
12 times 3 is Even Stevens...
Hawthorn blossom is called Even Stevens...

Some of his mates were really jealous.

I'm better at football than you, Wayne. I ought to be playing for the Stevens.

Maybe, you are but you don't live at an even number in Shakespeare Street, do you? So, hard cheese!

In the sixth round Even Stevens were drawn at home to Aston Villa.

Now, you would probably agree that Even Stevens had had a bit of luck so far in the tournament. But what happened next was unheard of in the history of football.

Aston Villa got lost. That's right, lost.

That's hard luck on the Villa fans, Dad.

Football's a cruel game, son.

They just couldn't find their way to the Mammoth Hypermarket Astroturf.

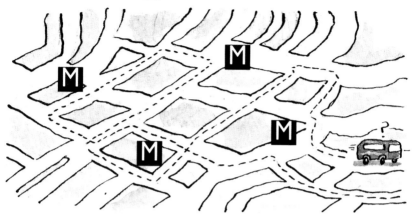

Perhaps the trouble was that Mammoth were doing rather good business and had opened up twelve new stores between Aston Villa and Hackney, but whatever it was, Villa never made it to the match.

Chapter 12

That week, Even Stevens trained hard.
Erkan had run out of ideas and the
intrepid team were just glad that they
had lasted long enough to meet such
brilliant opponents.

Even Stevens Team Photo

That week, Liverpool played hard.
On Monday they played Bayern
Munich in the fourth round of the
European Cup. It was a draw, replay
Thursday night.

On Tuesday they played in the fifth

round of the Humbellow Cup. It was a draw, replay Friday night.

On Thursday they played in the replay of the fourth round of the European Cup. It went to extra time. They lost.

On Friday they played in the replay of the fifth round of the Humbellow Cup. It went to extra time. They lost.

Liverpool Team Photo

Anyone could have beaten Liverpool that day.

Final score: Liverpool 0, Even Stevens 6.

Chapter 13

Yes, the amazing news was that Even
Stevens, the team from Shakespeare Street,
Hackney, were in the F.A. Cup Final.

The bad news was that
Nigel Fiddle was back from
Lithuania with another lot
of boots, and he wanted to play.

Wayne's dad's back was finally on the mend, too. Things didn't look good for Wayne.

At last the great day arrived.

4 MINS

…Spurs launch an attack down the middle. Sparrow sprays it out on the right flank to Doddle. A beautiful cross; it's beaten Rodney Travis! Greyleg has run through to nod it in. 1-nil to Tottenham, but there was a suspicion of off-side. Let's look at it again on the replay… and yes, definitely offside… Bobby?

Absolutely

...Doddle jinxing his way round the Stevens' defence. Postlethwaite's got it back, and, oh, that's a foul surely? Referee waves play on. Doddle takes it on the left foot. Top corner. It's a goal! 2-nil to Tottenham. Let's look at that again on the replay... and yes. that's a foul, surely... Bobby?

Absolutely

HACKNEY
SOCIAL CLUB

Foul!

Foul!

43 MINS

Greyleg takes the corner, and it's Doddle with the diving header. Fantastic save by Bradley. No! The referee's given a goal! Let's look at that again. Oh no, you can see Bradley held it. Oh dear me, the third controversial goal, Bobby...

Absolutely

Second half
51 MINS

...And Travis is down!

You can't let family feelings get in the way of football.

Bring Wayne on, Tesco...

...But I've sprained my eyelash!

... and Wayne Travis is on. Eyebulge towers over him, but Travis gets it away. Extraordinary – it's turning towards the penalty area. It's heading for goal. Spreadeagle's got it covered... Oh, no he hasn't. It's in! It's a goal! That's 3-1 to Spurs. The pitch must be a little uneven today, Bobby?

Absolutely

HACKNEY OLD FOLKS HOME

Goal!

Goal!

...Donna Louis fairly steaming through mid-field there. Travis takes it. Oh, it's a tame one. Bounces early, takes a strange turn. Slug's covering – he's misjudged it. Greyleg will clear off the line, surely... No – it's in. It's a goal! Sensational! 3-2.
The referee ought to look at the stitching on the ball, don't you agree, Bobby?

Absolutely

The seconds were ticking away. The ref
was looking at his watch. If only
Wayne could get the ball once more.

As the ref put the whistle in his mouth,
Satoshi slipped Wayne the ball.

Wayne took a huge swipe at it.
Off it went. One bounce, two bounces,
three bounces.
      It was going to be a goal…
            It was going to be the equaliser…

…Then the whistle went.
Half a second later the ball was in the net.
Goal but no goal.
            No extra time.
                  End of the game.
Spurs had won the cup.

Then an odd thing happened. Instead of letting the losing team collect their medals, the Spurs captain ran up to collect the F.A. Cup. He brought it back down to the pitch and gave Erkan the lid.

You were robbed, mate.

What a gesture, Bobby.

Absolutely

Chapter 14

Everyone agreed it was the most extraordinary F.A. Cup Final in football history. People all over the world argued about that final score.

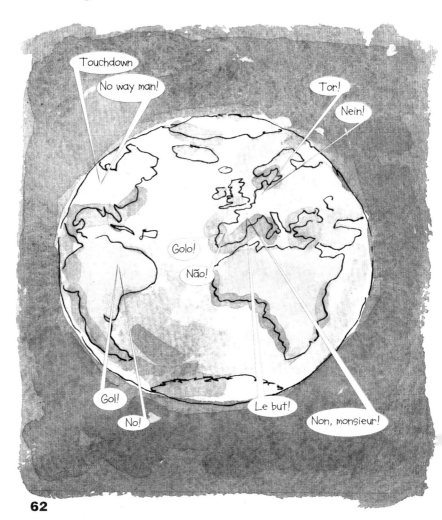

Wayne finally got his wish and appeared on the new *Goals of the Century* video.

And today people still study Wayne's kicks to see exactly what happened. The argument rages.

But Wayne Travis and the Even Stevens
F.C. squad will never forget that day.